I ADULTED
AT WORK!

I DIDN'T GET FIRED!

I WAS NICE TO THE NEW GUY!

I TRANSFERRED A CALL!

I WENT OUT FOR LUNCH!

I stopped for lunch!

I FIXED my BOSS'S MISTAKE!

I DIDN'T HAVE TO WORK LATE!

I DIDN'T KEEP PEOPLE IN THE WAITING ROOM!

I refilled the printer with PAPER!

I UNMUTED BEFORE SPEAKING!

I left Happy Hour early!

MY CAT DIDN'T WALK IN FRONT OF MY SCREEN!

I kept the TV off during work hours!

I didn't correct the GRAMMAR in your email!

I didn't correct MY BOSS in public!

I GOT PAID!

I CONNECTED TO THE SERVERS!

I MADE IT to FRIDAY!

I FILLED OUT my TIME SHEET!

I SURVIVED A WORK TRIP WITH MY BOSS

I CHANGED OUT OF MY PAJAMAS!

I watered the office plants!

I HELD THE ELEVATOR!

I wore PANTS during the video conference

I GOT A PROMOTION!

I took notes!

I BACKED UP MY OPINION WITH DATA!

I cleaned up my mess in the kitchen!

I AVOIDED MY BOSS all day!

I WORKED FROM HOME!

I FILED EVERYTHING CORRECTLY!

I HAVEN'T USED ALL MY VACATION DAYS!

I WAS WELL-LIT ON MY VIDEO CONFERENCE!

I'M TEAM BUILDING!

I FOUND THE EMAIL I WAS LOOKING FOR

I ADULTED AT WORK!

ESSENTIAL STICKERS

for HARDWORKING and HOME-WORKING

GROWN-UPS

Robb Pearlman

UNIVERSE

First published in the
United States of America in 2021 by
Rizzoli International Publications, Inc.
300 Park Avenue South
New York, NY 10010
www.rizzoliusa.com

Copyright © 2021 Robb Pearlman

Publisher: Charles Miers
Editor: Jessica Fuller
Design: Celina Carvalho
Managing Editor: Lynn Scrabis
Production Manager: Colin Hough-Trapp

Printed in China

2023 2024 2025 / 10 9 8 7 6 5

ISBN: 978-0-7893-3975-1
Library of Congress Control Number: 2020942155

Visit us online:
Facebook.com/RizzoliNewYork
Twitter: @Rizzoli_Books
Instagram.com/RizzoliBooks
Pinterest.com/RizzoliBooks
Youtube.com/user/RizzoliNY
Issuu.com/Rizzoli

After Monday and Tuesday,
even the calendar says WTF.

—Anonymous

YOU'RE AN ADULT—NOW GET TO WORK!

As an adult, you can do whatever you like. Stay up all night, sleep late, have cereal for dinner—which is great! But if you do stay up all night and sleep late, you may lose your job, in which case you'll *have* to have cereal for dinner—which isn't so great.

Because part of being an adult is having a job so you can pay for all the things kid-you dreamed of adult-you having and doing. It's . . . it's not always fun.

Work is literally, and I mean "literally" in both the literal and figurative sense, a four-letter word. Of course, finding a line of work you feel passionate about is a wonderful thing. There are many construction workers, first responders, accountants, coaches, administrative assistants, mechanics, servers, educators, and frontline workers who not only enjoy what they do for a living but feel an incredible amount of satisfaction and purpose in their work.

At the minimum, having a job you don't dread is the goal.

But sometimes circumstances or fate may put you in a position to take, well, a position just to get by. Which sucks. Regardless of your job, you should be acknowledged for doing it well. That's where these stickers come in!

So even if you don't get praise, a raise, or are even told you're "lucky you still have a job during this economy," these stickers are easy ways to reward yourself, or your co-workers, for a job well-done. Literally.

Coworkers are like Christmas lights. They hang together, half of them don't work, and the other half aren't so bright."

—Anonymous

Bob Porter: Looks like you've been missing a lot of work lately.
Peter: I wouldn't say I've been missing it, Bob.

—*Office Space*

IT'S ME?

Though the level of weirdness may vary, every workplace has a weird person. Not evil or creepy or bad, just . . . weird. You know what I'm talking about. The person who can be counted on not only to hit "reply all" but do it on every single email they ever reply to. The person who will purposefully spill coffee on their keyboards to wipe up the bagel crumbs they've dropped into the crevices between the letters. The person who stinks up the entire place by cooking fish in the microwave in the break room. The person who takes off all of their clothing in the restroom.

Though they're sometimes difficult to spot, if, after serious thought, you can't easily identify the "weird" coworker, then I'm sorry to say that it's you, dear reader. You're the weird one.

You're also automatically the weird one if you work from home. Don't believe me? Ask the dog. *He* knows what you do. Weirdo.

I'M NOT INTO POLITICS

E ven if you don't work in an office, or in politics, you're going to encounter "office politics" in every job you have.

If you treat the person who empties the recyclables with the same respect you treat the person in the corner office, you're off to a good start, but you do need to remember that not everyone will adhere to these rules.

You may find yourself in the middle of a he-said-he-said between coworkers, a she-said-she-said between superiors, or even a he-said-it-said between that weird guy in the office who now sits on a foam doughnut and the "mystery" as to why the copy machine has a butt-shaped indentation in its glass.

And even though spreading gossip around an office can be as satisfying as schmearing cream cheese on an everything bagel, the less you say about what you hear will keep you out of any other hearsay that's said or heard.

A lot of fellows nowadays have a B.A., M.D., or Ph.D. Unfortunately, they don't have a J.O.B.

—Fats Domino

DON'T STRESS! IT'S NOT BRAIN SURGERY!

Unless you're a brain surgeon, of course, in which case you should skip ahead. OK, now just between us non-first responders, you should know your work is not, and should not, define your life. Nor should it stress you out so completely that it ruins it.

"One of the symptoms of an approaching nervous breakdown is the belief that one's work is terribly important."

—Bertrand Russell

> "I work for myself, which is fun. Except when I call in sick, I know I'm lying."
>
> —Rita Rudner

It's human nature for people to want to feel proud of their productivity, but if you don't at least try to maintain a healthy balance between work and real life, you're going to be an empty husk of a person. Make sure to set boundaries with your coworkers—and especially your boss—regarding when and how you're available to them. Set ground rules as to whether or not it's appropriate and necessary to get and reply to texts and emails after normal work hours, on holidays, or weekends. It's up to you to make sure you're not being taken advantage of, but it's also up to you to make sure that you're giving yourself enough downtime to recharge and recommit to your job.

If you wind up living to work, rather than working to live, you'll quickly find yourself isolated from the family, friends, and activities that you no longer have time for.

JUST DO IT

As charming as it may have been putting the "pro" in procrastination during your time in school, your lackadaisical ways will do you no favors once you get a job. Your coworkers, bosses, clients, and customers are all counting on you to do your job—and do it well.

Whether you're a cog in a corporate machine, a freelancer, or a boots-on-the-ground tradesperson, by accepting a job you're accepting the responsibility to do your best (or at least not do your worst) in accomplishing the tasks at hand. And as good as coasting by to complete an assignment may feel, it's actually going to feel even better if you feel like you've done it to the best of your ability.

So even though an assigned task can be challenging or boring or repetitive or seemingly meaningless or inconsequential or even just interfering with your side hustle or efforts to get concert tickets before they sell out, remember that you're being paid to actually do something, not just collect a paycheck.

Hard work never
killed anybody, but why
take a chance?

—Edgar Bergen

The best way to appreciate your job is to imagine yourself without one.

—Oscar Wilde

I DIDN'T **FALL ASLEEP** DURING THE CONFERENCE

I DIDN'T >>> HIT "REPLY ALL"!

I CLEARED MY INBOX!

I REMEMBERED THE INTERN'S NAME!

I didn't spread **OFFICE GOSSIP!**

I heard **EVERYONE** *on a* conference call*!*

I BACKED UP MY OPINION **WITH DATA!**

I **HELPED** ⬛*a*⬛ **COWORKER** **!**

I cleaned my keyboard!

I **CHANGED** *the* **TONER**

MY CAT DIDN'T WALK IN FRONT OF MY SCREEN!

I stopped for lunch!

I WORKED FROM HOME!

I WORKED FROM HOME!

I WORKED FROM HOME!

I STAYED UNDER BUDGET!

I got a raise! *

I didn't ~~correct~~ MY BOSS in public!

I MADE A SENSIBLE CHOICE! ✓

I HELD THE ELEVATOR !

I FILED
EVERYTHING
CORRECTLY
!

I AVOIDED
A POLITICAL
DISCUSSION
!

I
cleaned up
my mess
in the
kitchen!

*I
MADE IT
to
FRIDAY
!*

*I
MADE IT
to
FRIDAY
!*

I CRUNCHED NUMBERS!

I GOT A  PROMOTION!

I HAVEN'T USED ALL MY VACATION DAYS!

I didn't wait until the LAST MINUTE!

I WENT OUT FOR LUNCH!

MY EXCEL FORMULAS WORKED!

I watered the office plants!

I WAS PRODUCTIVE TODAY!

I WAS PRODUCTIVE TODAY!

I WAS PRODUCTIVE TODAY!

I DIDN'T MAKE A **BIG DEAL** OUT OF IT!

I **WAS NICE** TO THE NEW GUY!

I finished on time !

I didn't drink TOO MUCH at the holiday PARTY!

I WORKED **ALL** WEEKEND !

I kept the **TV** off during work hours!

I returned a **PHONE CALL!**

I WAS **ON TIME** FOR A **MORNING MEETING!**

I WAS **ON TIME** FOR A **MORNING MEETING!**

I WAS **ON TIME** FOR A **MORNING MEETING!**

IT'S CASUAL FRIDAY!

I SURVIVED A WORK TRIP WITH MY BOSS !

I REALLY WAS SICK !

I KNOW WHAT I'M DOING!

I aced my review!

I'M TEAM BUILDING!

I CLEANED *my* CUBICLE !

I GAVE MONEY FOR SOMEONE'S BIRTHDAY CAKE!

I TOOK *the* STAIRS!

my **PowerPoint** *was on* **point** !

I didn't **ROLL MY EYES** *during the video conference* **!!**

I DIDN'T KEEP PEOPLE IN THE **WAITING ROOM!**

I CHANGED OUT OF MY PAJAMAS !

I CHANGED OUT OF MY PAJAMAS !

I CHANGED OUT OF MY PAJAMAS !

I listened
to my
voicemail!

I WAS
WELL-LIT
ON MY VIDEO
CONFERENCE!

MY DOG MADE
EVERYONE SMILE!

I
CONNECTED
TO THE
SERVERS!

I
chose a good
VIRTUAL
background
!

I DIDN'T WORK my SIDE HUSTLE DURING WORK!

I set up my home office!

I didn't correct the **GRAMMAR** in your email!

I REMOVED the PAPER JAM!

I asked for HELP!

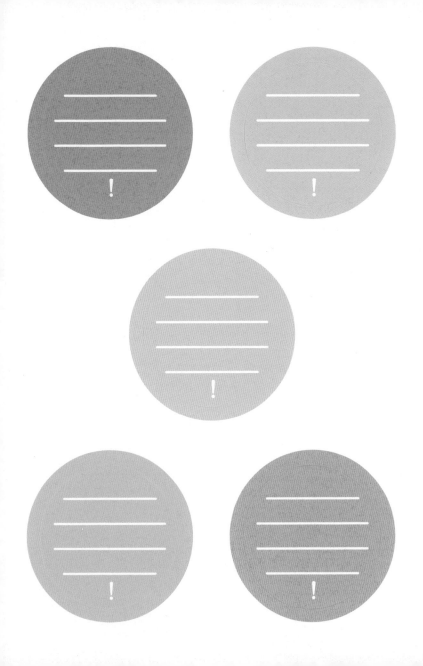